Almira Stillwell Cole

Six Days on the Hurricane Deck of a Mule

An Account of a Journey Made on Mule Back in Honduras, C.A. - 1891

Almira Stillwell Cole

Six Days on the Hurricane Deck of a Mule
An Account of a Journey Made on Mule Back in Honduras, C.A. - 1891

ISBN/EAN: 9783744744539

Printed in Europe, USA, Canada, Australia, Japan

Cover: Foto ©Andreas Hilbeck / pixelio.de

More available books at **www.hansebooks.com**

SIX DAYS ON THE HURRICANE DECK OF A MULE.

L AST spring I almost learned to ride a bicycle.

Those who have had a similar struggle will correctly estimate the exact value of that word *almost*. I was laboring under peculiar difficulties, for I was a whilom inmate of one of those sacred institutions—a young ladies' boarding-school,—where any infringement upon the Spartan law of dignity would have been looked upon as less pardonable than a simultaneous indulgence in the seven deadly sins.

My agony of mind and body under those circumstances can be better imagined than described. Methought life held no more painful experience, but how impossible it is to gauge endurance and classify suffering I have since learned.

When, later on, I announced to my friends and relatives my intention of taking up a residence in the interior of *Honduras* for the ensuing five years, I was fairly overwhelmed by the storm of exclamations, reproaches, dire predictions, and tearful expostulations, none of which shook my resolution.

I assured them that the trip was simple enough,—by steamer from *New York* to *Colon*, thence by rail to *Panama*, where a steamer was taken to *Amapala*, and then over the mountain on mule-back.

One friend in vain tried to move me by drawing dreadful pictures of life with a ruined complexion ; another assured me I was going to bury myself among barbarians; a third pointed out the miseries of sea-sickness and the certainty of death from some fever which would be sure to attack me at once, and so *ad infinitum*.

I bore it all as meekly as possible and with outward patience, but inward raging.

I told them I cared more for the complexion of my life than the amount of sun-kissed pigment my skin contained; I would civilize all the barbarians I found; and since others had endured sea-sickness so could I.

However, at last a teasing cousin did hit upon a fact, and a stubborn one, which had tormented me considerably—that mule I was to ride. He assured me that had I ever attempted to ride a wheel I would have some idea of what was in store for me. With a sinking heart but unabashed countenance, I smiled a superior sort of smile and replied that I had learned to ride a wheel.

"Well, a mule is worse," was the reply that somewhat staggered me.

Then I did not believe him, but now I think he must be divinely gifted with the spirit of prophecy.

Sailing day came, and with all the assurance and independence of a typical American young woman, I stood on the deck of a steamer alone, and watched the familiar faces of friends fade into the distance.

Sixteen days later, as I was about to go ashore in *Honduras*, I audibly wondered why any one should find the journey anything but delightful. Every moment had been an enjoyable one, and I had entirely escaped one of the foretold horrors. Imagine the shadow that crept across the sunshine of my mental vision, when the Captain of the ship I was leaving so regretfully remarked, with a wise and mysterious shake of his head :

"Perhaps you will see why, when you have been for six days on the hurricane deck of a mule."

A youth, considerably my junior, whom I had known well as a schoolboy in the States, had come with two men-servants and six mules to meet me. As I stood on shore and watched the vessel steam out of the harbor, I did almost feel as if I had had my final contact with civilization.

We went at once to the hotel, which I thought the dirtiest place I had ever seen.

Since then I have learned to discriminate nicely between different degrees of filth.

Here we were obliged to remain for two days, for *Amapala* is on an island, and one has to be transported to the mainland before the journey can be continued. The little steamer does not run regularly, as *mañana* is the same as to-day, if not preferable, to the native of the coast.

We could hardly believe the evidence of our senses when finally we were plowing our way over the bay toward our desired destination, some two and a half hours after the proprietors of the launch had assured us they would be ready to start.

In all the heat of the tropical noonday sun we came to a stop two hours later, at *La Brea*, and alighted upon a sandy beach, back of which were a store-house and a few small mud cabins. In the office of the store-house we ate our lunch, and shortly after word came to me that the fated moment for mounting had arrived.

With a heart beating with apprehension I went outside where I found quite a group of curious natives, while in the midst stood the antagonist with whom I was to wage such an unaccustomed warfare—a gentle-looking beast, gayly trapped out in a handsome saddle of red and tan leather, under which was a corresponding velvet cloth.

With a degree of satisfaction somewhat reassuring, I noted that she was large enough to carry me and yet so small that a fall from her height could not be wholly fatal. What I further noticed and was troubled by was the fact that the saddle was made for the right side instead of the left, and then it was borne in upon my mind, that the hope that a slight experience on horseback ten years before would prove of some service to me now, was a perfectly futile one. I was about to embark upon an unknown sea, with no chart to guide me in its navigation.

Meanwhile a low chair had been brought, upon which I climbed preparatory to making the further ascent. Just then my courage was at such a low ebb that to take the next step seemed beyond me.

" Vincent, I can't do it."

"You must," was the unsympathizing reply, and seeing me still hesitate, he added : " You can't walk, and this is the only way."

That settled it. In sheer despair, I set my teeth together, shut my eyes and jumped, remembering that " whatever goes up must come down "—somewhere, and I did not much care where.

Even yet I retain more than a vivid memory of the astonishment I felt when I discovered that I had actually alighted in the right place. My stock of self-esteem has been on the increase ever since.

In a few moments we started merrily off, I soon becoming used to the motion, and rather liking it. If only my cousin could have witnessed my triumph, my happiness would have been complete.

The road lay over a velvety plain, and for a couple of hours we rode on, the only incident at all exciting, being an effort on my part to leave my head perched upon a heavy limb of an overhanging tree. This

danger past, no new danger presented itself
to disturb our quiet progress, and toward
the end of the afternoon, we rode into
Nacaome, the little village where we were
to spend the night.

Dismounting at the entrance to an *adobe*
house, with doors standing hospitably ajar,
we were bidden to enter, and were shown
into a great bare room, with a tiled floor, no
ceiling except the roof of tiles, and containing two chairs, two beds, and a table. There
were no windows, two great doors, one on
each side of the corner, admitting light and
air, and at one side of the room a smaller
door led into another apartment, for this
was a house on an unusual scale.

The native bed is something unique, and
perhaps a description of it will not come
amiss. A plain, high, single wooden bed-
stead, such as we sometimes see in very
old-fashioned farm-houses, first has ropes
or strips of skin drawn over it, upon which
is placed a piece of matting, or in some
cases, leather—the latter a sign of luxury.

During the day it presents this appearance, but at night a hard pillow is added, the native woman wraps herself in a sheet, and lies down on the matting to sleep as peaceful and dreams as blissful, let us hope, as her more favored sister who reclines upon a downy couch under a silken coverlid.

I had no occasion to test the comfort of this bed in its primitive state, for our servants had brought with them everything that could render our quarters bearable if there were any foundation upon which to build.

A hammock was slung up in the room, and I found I had never before cherished a proper appreciation of one. Even a summer girl, with all the romantic accessories of "shady nook, babbling brook," and so on, can form no conception of the soul-satisfying comfort derived from abandoning oneself to the luxurious embrace of a hammock, after a few hours' ride on a mule. One friend who had survived the experience I was just beginning, had warned me not to think death was nigh at the end of the first day, so I lay there almost vainly trying to convince myself that these were only natural and ordinary sensations and would not bring about a general dissolution.

Thus reflecting I fell into a kind sleep, from which I was aroused by a terrific clap of thunder and such a deluge of rain as I had never witnessed. Heretofore I had always disliked lightning, but nature's present "pyrotechnical display" challenged naught but my most enthusiastic admiration. When it was over supper was announced, and soon afterward we retired for the night, I occupying one of the beds in the big room, one of the women of the house the other, and poor Vincent being relegated to a hammock swung up in the next room, where the entire family—men, women, and children—slept.

I was soon oblivious to my surroundings, and, in the style of the chroniclers, thus endeth the history of the first day.

Upon awaking the following morning, I found I was considerably rested, and quite willing to undertake a continuance of the journey, for which a specially glorious day seemed promised.

About half past seven we were off, I having mounted my steed with a little more agility than before. Indeed, I improved so rapidly in this respect before the trip was over, that my companion, in a burst of boyish enthusiasm, gave it as his opinion that I could "earn five dollars a day in Buffalo Bill's show." What untold wealth might now have been mine had not this talent so long lain dormant!

About half a mile from our starting-point we came to a river which at this place had divided itself, forming two forks, and both had become so swollen during the present rainy season that it seemed a serious matter to ford them, especially when my inexperience was taken into consideration.

An Indian, who lived on the bank, when drawn into the consultation advised us to go farther down and cross the big river in a canoe. We went, he acting as our guide, and when we came to the place where the canoe ought to be, behold, it was on the other side of the stream.

Then ensued such a series of screeches and yells as made me tremble for the safety of my scalp and look furtively around for a score of blood-thirsty natives to spring from ambush, but when my fears were somewhat calmed I understood that our guide was merely calling to the boatman across the way.

His efforts met with no success, and with a stream of eloquence which my limited knowledge of profanity would never allow me to translate into plain English, he rolled up his trousers, grabbed the halter of my mule, and without further ado plunged into the water and made for the other shore.

Sometime I will put it on record for how long it is possible to hold one's breath. During the time we were slipping and sliding over the stones, sometimes finding a foothold almost an impossibility and with difficulty breasting the current, I had no use whatever for oxygen, but lived wholly upon terror and the thought of a watery

grave. Such was not to be my fate, however, and I escaped to endure greater
trials and revel in far more wonderful
experiences.

After reaching *terra firma*, on and on we
rode over a plain similar to the one we had
traversed the previous afternoon. Once
we came to a tiny stream flowing across
our path, so small it was hardly worth
noticing, but to my surprise my mule objected so seriously and so suddenly to
wetting her feet, that I was nearly un-
seated, and in consequence was led to
investigate the cause of her conduct. I
somewhat sympathized with her when I
found that the pretty light blue rivulet was
formed of steaming hot water, the outlet
of a boiling spring hard by. In time my
superior will conquered, and we crossed
the water, which is so hot that eggs can be
cooked in it.

As we were riding along in silence, I
watching the many-colored lizards darting
from our vicinity, marvelling at the size
attained by the cactus in its native clime,

and indulging in many comparisons, *not* odious, I was suddenly startled by a most outrageous din apparently proceeding from a clump of trees just before us—such groans and shrieks as if all civilized creation were yielding up the ghost in the last throes of mortal agony for the special delectation of innumerable cannibals, whose cries and yells of evident delight could also be plainly heard.

Terror-stricken, I glanced at my companion, but he seemed perfectly undisturbed.

"What is it?" I managed to hoarsely whisper.

" Wagons," he briefly ejaculated.

And wagons I found it to be of a kind and class utterly unknown to me. The wheels were slices of trees, cut diametrically, in the centre of which holes had been bored for the insertion of the axles.

I think in order to fully accomplish the feat of making this a two-wheeled cart, and a music box combined, they must have used kerosene oil for axle grease. So

much for the sound of concentrated human
woe which I must eternally regret Milton
could not have heard before he described
the sufferings of the lost souls in purgatory.
The cries of fiendish joy were only the
loving words of cheer addressed by the
charioteers to the patient oxen drawing the
creaking, rumbling, rolling wagons on over
the rough, uneven roads.

Gladly we passed them by and as quickly
as possible got beyond earshot.

At noon the servants had not yet over-
taken us, and as we were fairly famished, we
stopped at an Indian hut along the way,
to partake of any hospitality the place
might afford.

It did not look particularly inviting, I
must confess. An old man, whose whole
attire consisted of a pair of trousers and a
hat, sat outside the door, the centre of a
more or less scantily clad group of women
and children, while around all, caloes, pigs,
chickens, ducks, and cats ran riot.

I must say for the Indian of *Honduras*
that no matter what his degree of filth,

poverty, nakedness, or intelligence, he never hesitates for one instant to take in a stranger and share with him all that he has.

It was, perhaps, this novel and spontaneous kindness added to my more than perfect willingness to endure a restful separation from my mule, which induced me to get down and enter that house with all my inborn and inbred love of cleanliness and daintiness crying out within me.

Only one door led into the one room containing beds, table, chair, boxes, and oh, bliss! a hammock, which, dirty as it was, I was only too thankful to occupy. No window lighted the darkness of the place, or afforded an occasional breath of fresh air. The floor was packed earth and was so dirty that it was a perfect paradise for swarms of fleas and other insects.

Vincent shot a chicken, which one of the women cooked—a proceeding which an Indian woman can accomplish with greater celerity and success than any I have hitherto encountered. This fowl was simply delicious, and, with boiled eggs and *tortillas* in addition, served as an admirable means of refreshing our starving bodies, and we partook of all heartily, in spite of the more than unappetizing surroundings.

After our mules had finished their repast of cut grass, we proceeded on our route. Considering the avidity with which the harmless-looking little insects, known here as *pulgas*, had seized upon me as a new and delicious morsel upon which to prey, I was not sorry to flee from them, and the motion of the mule seemed to allay the horrible irritation which I could only locate as "all over."

During the afternoon we just skirted the town of *Pespire*, and then passed into shady lanes which wound in and out a country gradually becoming more undulating.

It was not a great while before we discovered that a sudden shower, so common in tropical countries, was upon us, and in all probability we had before us the pleasant prospect of a drenching.

We were not wrong in our guess, for the water, ere many moments had passed, came down in torrents. With one hand I held my umbrella and so protected my head and shoulders, and with the other guided my mule.

Before the rain ceased we came to a house where Vincent informed me we would find our quarters until morning.

Three women sat in front of the house, under shelter of the projecting roof, one smoking a cigarette and the other two shelling corn. A hammock was hung here, and two chairs, a bench, and a table completed the furniture of this outside room.

Mules, pigs, dogs, and chickens roamed at will in the yard directly in front, which was muddy and shiny, and reeking with filth.

My heart sank lower than ever within me, but summoning up what I could of my resolution to bear uncomplainingly whatever came, I got off my mule, stiff, lame, wet, and cold, and sat down in the hammock, wondering how much more I could endure.

We had not seen our servants since morning, and were becoming somewhat anxious, remembering the river and the rain, but still found consolation in the thought that the heavily laden pack mules could not travel as fast as we had done.

Hardly had we settled ourselves under this shelter when a man rode up, apparently "the lord of the manor." He was about fifty years of age, whiter than the women, and was getting a horrible *goitre*, an affliction that one of the girls, his daughter, was also suffering from, and which seemed quite a common one in the vicinity.

A few words of explanation from the pretty cigarette-smoker, who, though not his wife, seemed to be the mistress of the household, apparently satisfied him, and he subsequently took our presence as a matter of course.

He seated himself in the chair by the table, his supper of black beans, meat, cheese, and *tortillas* was brought and dispatched without the aid of either knife or fork, and then he turned his attention to our entertainment.

Notwithstanding the unwelcome sights and odors, we were becoming very hungry again, and as our men still abstained from putting in an appearance, we were more than glad to take the eggs, *tortillas*, and coffee given us. True it is that oftentimes during that six days, I ate and relished such food in places where, under ordinary circumstances, I would not have tasted a mouthful of the most tempting delicacies.

About dark one of the men came with three of the mules, but the other man had lost himself in trying to find us, and not until several hours later did he succeed in his quest.

Meanwhile I was secretly tormented by the painful anxiety to know where I was to sleep. One dark, ill-smelling room was all the house contained, except a shed used as a kitchen, and I could not see how the most ingenious hostess could make two guests of different sexes comfortable, however much she might incommode the family.

To my utter horror I learned that, with no conception of any possible scruples on my part, she had arranged for me to have one of the four beds, the women of the house the remaining three, while the master and Vincent were to occupy hammocks in the same room.

With stoical disregard of masculine observance, these native families disrobed themselves, skilfully it is true, though the process of necessity was a short one, and then, in company with their male companion, deliberately set themselves to watch my preparations for the night.

These last, you may be sure, were of the simplest kind. I took off my shoes and let down my hair, and then in my still wet dress, which was fortunately a flannel one, I crept into the bed the servant had made up with the clothes we carried with us.

Vincent's night toilet was still less elaborate.

He unbuckled the leather belt upon

which hung his revolver, and brought it over to me with a brief injunction that I was to use it if need be. A startling suggestion truly, but the weapon gave me a sense of security, though it was such an enormous one that I knew with both hands on the trigger, both eyes tight shut, and mouth firmly set in the usual feminine way, I could never make the thing go off, in time to render me more than a *post-mortem* defence.

As the burning pine sticks which had furnished light for us, slowly crumbled into ashes, I heard a wonder-struck voice ask if all the American ladies went to bed with their clothes on, to which Vincent, sharing my desire to do or say nothing that could hurt their feelings, gravely replied that it was the national custom.

Of course I did not sleep, tired as I was —I was more than half afraid to close my eyes, and when I finally did summon up sufficient courage to do so, there ensued a series of disturbances that successfully banished any further somnolent inclination for the night.

First our man, Eduardo, arrived, and all the animals about felt it their bounden duty to extend to him a welcome, whence began a simultaneous barking of dogs, mewing of cats, grunting of pigs, crowing of roosters, quacking of ducks, braying of mules, neighing of horses, and wagging of tongues, as I had never heard since in my childish days we had " lived on my father's farm in the green fields of barley."

When that commotion had subsided, our host sank into slumber so noisy that I lay there in momentary expectation of seeing the roof depart upon a celestial journey, and I am sure it was only saved from displacement by the rebellion of his throat causing a terrific fit of coughing. This over, he recounted a vivid, if stupid dream he had just had, and then once more came restful silence.

It was not to last long, however, for in the early dawn a neighbor rode over to help kill a pig, but after a lengthy debate, it was decided that *mañana* would do as well.

By this time the farm world was astir, and we were not long in following suit. So, tired, dirty, still damp from yesterday's rain, I arose to meet the trials and tribulations of the third day.

Two little facts came to my knowledge before our simple breakfast, which gave a new color to my thoughts and revived my drooping spirits.

One was a prospect of absolute cleanliness, for Vincent told me they had a bathroom in their house, a luxury I must confess I had not expected to find in a small village in interior *Honduras*.

At *Amalapa* I had most regretfully said good-by to two good steamer friends who were going to the capital by another road, and one which led through *Pespire*, the little village we had passed the previous afternoon.

As good luck would have it, Eduardo, in his wanderings, had gone to a sort of agency there to inquire if we had been seen, and had found a letter for me, left by one of the two travellers who had preceded us. Surely never a communication from the dearest friend I had ever had was quite so eagerly seized and devoured as was this brief note, which came to me like a refreshing glimpse of the world I had known. Heaven bless the writer for his kindly inspiration !

At eight o'clock we were again mounted, and had said good-by for ever, I trust, to *San Juan*. Oh, mockery of names! Meanwhile my companion had informed me that we would soon come to the mountains, where I knew I should meet the much-talked-of equestrian difficulty.

We had not ridden long before it seemed to me our road came to a sudden termination, for right before us rose a steep and rocky cliff. Too soon I learned that we must scale this ; so grasping my saddle firmly, I prepared to hang on while the mule did the rest. Just in the worst part of it, I became aware that the saddle was turning, and no effort or skill of mine could save me from a fall. Vincent saw my danger and shouted to me to jump, at the same time dismounting and hurrying to my assistance. With all too brief a prayer for mercy, I let go of everything except the bridle, and landed a shapeless mass, fortunately one containing considerable adipose, directly under the mule and upon a bed of jagged rocks.

My mule, bless her heart! never stirred, or I should either have had my head crushed by her hoofs, or have been hurled into the depths below.

As it was I was only slightly bruised, and very shaky, but as soon as the saddle was righted and firmly fastened, I was ready to mount and go on.

Then I was not so anxious for my cousin's presence, though Vincent will bear me witness that it was no fault of mine.

I learned during the day that the Spanish word for road is a most expansive one. For miles we went up and down over smooth, glaring white rocks, where no animal on earth but a Honduras mule could have found a footing. When I saw any particularly rugged bit of scenery, a gorge, a cliff, where surely human foot had never trod, I was told it was the road. I never foresaw where we were going for one instant. I kept the reins in my hand, but never pretended to guide the animal, whose intelligence I now had to admit was superior to my own. When we were going along the brinks of precipices so frightful that I dared not look over, I fixed my eyes upon the ears wagging so complacently before me, and imbibed courage therefrom.

Withal I was a trifle amused at the conviction that I, who had hitherto not quite entirely trusted any one, not even a man, was now abandoning myself to a most consuming confidence in a mule.

On in this way we went for six mortal hours, through pine forests with the trees so far apart that we got no shade, over the white rocks that nearly blinded us, and with the sun pouring down upon us in midday fury.

Then we began to ascend an almost perpendicular peak.

When little more than half-way up, a

mule and driver came suddenly around a sharp turn and so startled my hitherto gentle animal that, with a snort of rage, she jumped from the path and bounded from rock to rock of the cliff above, I meanwhile clinging to her like a burr, and momentarily expecting to roll with her into the ragged gully hundreds of feet below.

But again I was doomed to happy disappointment, for a final effort carried us over a particularly dangerous projection, and the next instant we were on a plain and only a few rods from *La Breita*, our stopping-place.

I scarcely remember how I dismounted. I know it was with great difficulty that I got myself straightened from a sitting posture, and entered a house so cool and clean that I thought I must have unwittingly stumbled into Paradise. It goes without saying that I was soon in a hammock, trying amid those comfortable surroundings to forget how every bone and muscle ached, how a combination of sleeplessness, continued fasting, and the glaring roadway was tending to bring on a fearful headache, and that there were still three days of the journey ahead of me.

However, by the time I had eaten some lunch I felt better, and began to take an interest in my surroundings.

The house, of course, was one of the class Bret Harte describes as "those queer little adobe buildings, with tiled roofs like longitudinal slips of cinnamon," and belonged to a well-to-do family, the head of which was a large mule owner, who had amassed his wealth in carrying cargoes from the coast to the interior.

He was not at home, so his wife, two daughters, a servant, and a half-foolish boy of eighteen or nineteen, were the only inmates of the house.

On this particular afternoon they were entertaining three girl friends—the two younger ones being pretty, and naturally clad in the costume of their race, while the older one had unfortunately become imbued with some so-called civilized ideas regarding her toilet.

A calico dress of the most painfully intense pink was made with a full, plain skirt and an ill-fitting basque, which failed to accomplish a meeting with the skirt at the usual trysting-place. Over this she had a shawl of the most royal shade of purple imaginable, and instead of looking like a pretty, graceful Indian girl, she appeared to be a variegated monstrosity.

I feel self-reproached at criticising her thus, for she, with the other two visitors, admired me intensely, and when sufficient time had elapsed for them to conquer their bashfulness, they asked Vincent, in hushed and reverent tones, if all the ladies in the States were so "tall, and nice, and white, and beautiful."

I had previously known that I was tall and could be nice when occasion demanded it, but it required the elastic conscience and easily aroused admiration of a warmer-blooded race than mine, to find whiteness or beauty in the face of an ordinary, typical, American brunette.

They departed before dark, and with

dark came a return of the perplexity regarding the sleeping accommodations I had experienced at *San Juan.*

In the large room—the living room—there were two beds, a hammock, some chairs, two tables, and—a " New Home " sewing-machine!   Off one end of this there was a small apartment also containing two beds, and separated from the larger one by a board partition perhaps six or seven feet high.

In my inmost heart I longed for the privacy of this narrow space, but such was not in accordance with our hostess' idea of hospitality.   I was assigned to a bed covered by a crucifix-surmounted canopy, in the main room, and Vincent was invited to take the other.   Upon his modestly stating he would sleep somewhere in a hammock, the mistress told the foolish boy he could have that bed.   To this I objected, in English, and forthwith Vincent was led to change his mind and accept the previously refused favor.

While I was making my nocturnal preparations, complete enough to insure comfort, I remember lazily musing upon the horrified, scandalized countenances some good friends would present, could they know how easily I was discarding all previous teachings and traditions, and, without a struggle, embracing new creeds and customs. I recall that I realized it was my duty, as a properly reared product of civilization, to go out and sit on a fence, if need be, to maintain my maidenly isolation and dignity, but I was too tired.

It is not the first case on record when a willing spirit has been worsted by weak flesh in a moral combat.

I slept as long, blissfully, and dreamlessly, as if I had not the heinous crime of having defied Mrs. Grundy upon my conscience, and awoke on the morning of the fourth day feeling decidedly refreshed.

Before us lay the longest day's ride of all, so we were anxious to be off as early as possible. We had our breakfast of coffee and *rosquillas*, not a hearty repast, and prepared to mount.

After each female member of the household had minutely examined my dress, hat, gloves, and veil, and remarked thereon ; after Vincent had written down my name and had taught them to pronounce it, and had, in answer to their unresented inquiries, given them choice bits of my history ; after they had, it seemed to me, exhausted all their resources to detain us further, some one of them suddenly bethought herself of one of the fixtures of the machine, whose use they could not determine.

I think I sank in their estimation somewhat, because I could not enlighten them. I suggested hemmer, tucker, quilter, braider, ruffler, and every known attachment I could think of, but each was produced with a flourish that negatived every proposition.

I finally gave it up, but if the New Home Sewing Machine Co. will communicate with me, I will some time, for penance, make a journey to *La Breita*, and reinstate myself in the good graces of the kindly inhabitants thereof, by solving the mystery for them.

About half past seven we did get off, and could all the good wishes that were given us in parting come true, we would be more than mortally favored.

We had no rough roads to go over that day. Across grassy plains where hundreds of cattle were grazing ; through shady lanes that seemed like the picturesque bridle paths of carefully cultivated parks, we rode for four hours, and then reaching a decently clean house we stopped, the "inner man" having clamored for refreshment for some time.

We found a young girl here, taking care of two children for their absent father and mother, and not a thing did she feel like shouldering the responsibility of giving us but one wretched ear of roast corn. In vain we begged and offered enormous sums for just one of the many fowls running about,—she was not to be moved. In despair we disposed ourselves under a huge tree by the roadside to await the arrival of Eduardo.

I believe it was some two hours afterward that he came, just as we were going to cast lots as to who should devour the other. Right glad were we to substitute the appetizing lunch soon spread for us in true picnic style, and full justice did we show it.

It was not long before we were again on our way, feeling much better satisfied with ourselves and the world in general. What a cure for the "blues" a good square meal is!

Just before we reached a little town, *La Armenia*, we made a descent of some wonderful rocks. I looked back at them and wished I had a camera. I know a picture of them, with "Where did they come from?" written underneath, would bring me a small fortune as a copyrighted prize puzzle. No one but a mule could solve it; and after all that would be the best answer. I cannot do any better myself, even after having made the dizzy journey from top to bottom.

We trotted through *La Armenia* in our very best style—I, because I did not want to be unfavorably compared with an habitual mule-back performer,—Vincent, because, as he afterwards confided to me, one of the prettiest girls in all *Honduras* lived there.

The rest of the afternoon passed uneventfully enough. To reach *San Pedro* was the object of our exertion, and fondly I hoped the key-keeping saint would unlock some safe and savory abiding-place for our night's habitation.

About half after five I saw before us a church and a few small houses, and though I heard no crowing of cocks, a barking of dogs intimated that we had reached a village, none other than the namesake of Rome's favorite apostle.

At the farther end of the settlement we found our accommodations.

Outwardly considered these houses are much alike, and though the inside furniture is almost as similar in kind and disposition, the interiors do vary greatly after all.

As I lay in a hammock which had been put up for me in front of the house, and

watched the moon rise from behind a
mountain just across the road, it seemed
to me that life was very beautiful and well
worth living, in spite of all its hardships.
The higher the moon rose, the more fully
her glorious rays streamed over all the
surrounding objects and bathed them in a
more charitable light than anything feminine is supposed to do, the more nearly
romantic I grew and felt almost like finding a certain charm even in *San Juan*.
The announcement that my bed was
awaiting me was all that saved me from
utter lunacy. Casting a last lingering
glance upon the fair beauty of the scene
before me, I gathered together my half-
scattered prosaic faculties and went in-
doors to—can I ever give you an idea of it?

Across a vilely dirty room was stretched
a cord upon which were hung to dry, huge
and manifold strips of salt meat. To my
uneducated olfactories it seemed past the
turning point and far on the road to utter
ruin—the smell was so suffocating and
sickening.

One bed Eduardo had succeeded in making very comfortable for me, while on the other, in its birthday suit, lay an interesting but constantly wailing infant which was soon afterwards joined by its mother. A hammock for Vincent was here too, and shortly we were settled for the night in our several places.

I had expressed a preference to stay outside in my hammock, but the plan not proving a feasible one, I drenched a handkerchief with some perfumery, tied it under my nose, and tried to find relief in slumber sweet.

I was awakened by a queer sort of noise that made me feel creepy and afraid to breathe. I cannot describe it, for I do not know anything it was like. The darkness was so thick that I could cut it, I am sure, and the only certainty I felt at having found myself where I last remember having been, was the ever strengthening odor of that meat.

When I could bear the suspense no longer, in a frenzy of fear I broke the spell of silence and fairly shrieked to Vincent. I made known my woes ; he lighted a match, and there, just above my head, upon two pegs driven into the wall for that express use, sat two parrots dressing their feathers and making themselves both comfortable for the night and beautiful for the morrow. They looked as if they felt injured, and I know I did, at being thus disturbed.

The rest of the night passed somehow— the baby squalled, the parrots verbally expostulated, a hen in one corner of the room let her presence be known, a horrid cat under one of the beds joined in the performance, and the fleas grew more than lively, but the most potent factor was that too long-dead one which appealed to another sense than that of hearing.

How thankful I was when the dawn broke and I felt at liberty to release myself from the imprisonment I had for hours endured and go out into the fresh air. It was really cold I found, but soon after the sun climbed up over the mountain before us, we became aware that his genial rays were shedding comfortable warmth as well as benignant light upon all around.

We made an early start, as gladly saying good-by to *San Pedro* as we had regretfully bid farewell to *La Breita* the previous morning.

The road was a good one from a Honduranian standpoint, and the only novel feature of the landscape was the appearance of the rocks. The cliffs were black, and looked as if for centuries water had lashed in restless and often unsubdued fury around their bases, giving them that peculiar formation so well known to geologists.

All the plains were thickly strewn with black bowlders of sizes ranging from immensity to those applicable to building and paving purposes. Nowhere have I ever seen more convincing traces of the drift period.

As we were going over an open space where the sun shone more warmly than elsewhere, a great yellow and black snake lazily dragged itself across the road directly in front of me.

I was sorry to see it, not only because I have an innate loathing of anything that crawls in this smooth, sinuous, treacherous manner, but because I had wanted to make the journey without encountering a single experience of the kind.

According to our friend's representations, mostly derived from her imagination, aided by a school geography, the ground was fairly honeycombed with entrances to the abodes of these reptiles, and I fully expected to find them festooning trees, bushes, and fences, lying in wait within every tuft of grass, and in fact making my life one hideous, waking nightmare.

However, this was the first and, as was afterwards proved, the last creature of the kind I was called upon to view, either during my trip or my subsequent residence in the country up to the present time. Lizards I saw in plenty, but their shy, quick way of darting out of sight reminded me more of the bashful little squirrels at home than anything else. I really liked them, in their place of course.

It still lacked an hour of noon when we came to a running brook, upon whose bank grew a tree casting such an inviting shade that we could not resist its fascinations but dismounted, tied our mules, and began to wish and watch for the appearance of Eduardo.

Presently Vincent like

> " Zaccheus, he
> Did climb a tree."

the sooner to perceive the coming of the expected lunch, and I indulged in a nap. The approach of a horseman aroused me, and false hopes together, and also brought my companion to the ground.

The rider, a young, good-looking man, whose toilet was the nearest approach to a civilized one I had recently come across, despite his bare feet, to which were strapped spurs, drew up in the middle of the brook, and after the customary friendly greeting, proceeded to inspect us in a most leisurely way.

Time, a good deal of time, passed before our servant came, but there he sat. The lunch was spread and partaken of long and heartily, and still he calmly surveyed us, not at all in an impertinent way, but just as if he were honestly interested. We offered him some jelly, which he ate in a totally unabashed manner, but withdrew not his gaze. We ignored him, but he took not the hint. Stay there he did until we were remounted, and then for miles and miles he rode along with us.

We were rather amused than otherwise at his course, though perhaps we experienced a scarcely recognized feeling of relief when we came to a place where our roads lay in different directions. He shook hands with us in the same friendly, impressive, almost warm manner, and then galloped merrily off as if he had fulfilled an arduous duty and now felt as if he had a right to enjoy himself.

Shortly afterward we came to a height overlooking the *Yegnare Valley*, one of the most beautiful and far-reaching scenes it has ever been my good fortune to behold.

Great pointed peaks kiss the sky on

every side, and seem to shut out all the noise and strife of the world beyond, and like sentinels, grim and gaunt, guard intact the peace and prosperity of the vast plains within that natural wall.

Two farms occupy nearly all of the valley, and so extensive are they, that the farm-houses are four miles apart. The owner of both proved to be none other than the father of my companion, and though there was still one more day's journey before us, we already felt quite at home.

We made the descent and entered upon the broad domain of the *Hacienda de San Francisco*, the boundary of which, to my amazement, I found indicated by a very familiar American barb-wire fence.

We rode through fields where the grass waved high above our heads, over pasture plains where hundreds of cattle, mules, and horses roamed at will, and then, when the sun was sinking low, we came to the farm-house, and here we dismounted to make our last night's stop.

The building is a remarkable one, having been a monastery years and years ago, when the Jesuit missionaries were devoting their energies and lives to the conversion of the untamed Indians.

It is one hundred and fifty feet long, probably one third as deep, and has walls a yard thick. All this is divided into five rooms—three large ones running the whole depth of the house and communicating with each other, and two smaller ones, one behind the other, and only had access to from the outside.

The floors are of stone, and it pleased me to fancy that many of the worn places had been formed by constant contact with the bended knees of the holy and indefatigable priests. The projecting roof of tiles forms a sort of porch, we would call it, all around the building, and is paved, as is also the yard for many feet. Beyond this the land gently slopes to a river, and still farther on a mountain rises up to limit the landscape and prevent our greedy eyes from drinking of beauty to a more than endurable state of intoxication.

It was blissful to lie in a hammock and watch the setting sun give here and there a lingering farewell touch as if loath to go and leave behind so much that was beloved, and then at the close of the short tropical twilight to see fair Luna crown, first with a halo of approaching glory and then with her own sweet self, the dark peak whose outlines rose sharp and clear against the star-pierced blue of the evening sky.

It was blissful, I say, to revel in this grand pastoral poem in the full consciousness that the transition to prose would be one of terror ; to know that in one of the big, cool, clean rooms a comfortable bed was prepared for me, where I would lose myself in restful unconsciousness, guarded by the saint whose figure could be clearly defined in an old oil-painting on the wall, and which, with two others of a like kind, were relics, doubtless, of a chapel's previous decoration.

'T was even so, and when I awoke in the morning to find a huge vessel of water from the river standing by a shallow tub hewn from the trunk of a tree, while near at hand were placed all the articles necessary for body and soul-satisfying ablutions, my perfect content knew not how to manifest itself.

Beautiful *San Francisco!* What happiness to fill the house with twenty chosen friends and there to dream away a month or more of idle joy! Surely after such *dolce far niente* days life could hold no bitterness for which we had not, in experience, a ready antidote.

Too soon, it seemed, we were forced to leave there, for we had a long, weary day of mountain climbing ahead of us.

"A bad road," Vincent said, and when he warned me thus I knew I could expect the worst.

We departed through the fields again, past the barb-wire boundary line, across the river, and up among the foot-hills, leading to the mountain close at hand. When the topmost crest was reached I stopped for a last look at the *Yegnare Valley*, at *San Francisco* lying below, at *San*

Morano farther in the distance, at the mountain looming up in the background, beyond which lies *Tegacigalpa*, and then I turned with strengthened spirit to the task before me.

To my surprise, at this height we emerged from the woods, to find ourselves on a most extensive plain, very properly called, in the Spanish, *La Mesa*—the table. Here we encountered the wagon-road leading from the capital to our destination and for a long distance we followed it. After we left *La Mesa* it was simply horrible, and all my attention became absorbed in self.

By no means is any one to presume that my mule and I had become reconciled by our lengthened companionship. Discomfort amounting to positive agony had taught me to adopt more attitudes, graceful or ungraceful, than all the combined systems of Delsarte and other physical culturists could possibly suggest.

Every muscle in my body had been so frequently called into requisition that to use any one almost drew forth an involuntary scream. In various places the skin had been worn away by constant friction of the clothing or saddle, leaving highly sensitive sores, even my gauntlets reducing my wrists to such a state.

Words cannot express what I suffered. The torture had been of a less acute kind while we were riding over comparatively level roads, but here we were going " up hill and down dale " again, and how I was to bear it I could not see.

I tried to be brave, and I think rarely, if ever, a complaint passed my lips, but during that last day I more than once nearly committed suicide through sheer physical exhaustion.

My stock of reserved strength proved to be far greater than I had ever reason to believe it, and demand for more endurance was always met.

When my mule had some particularly difficult obstacle to surmount, she had a way of approaching it quietly and then suddenly giving a hump that filled her spine with complex curves and a burden, unless care were exercised, with compound fractures. In order to insure one's safety it is absolutely necessary to preserve an exact equilibrium directly over the said spine in a line running from the point midway between her ears to her tail. This is at times so gigantic a task that it is no wonder a temporary oblivion to bodily sensation is induced.

Poor mule! In moments when I could summon up any spare sympathy, I lavished it upon her. She seemed to be tired too.

Finally, when going down steep ravines, she ceased to lower herself and me gently from one foothold to the next, but acquired a habit of thumping down in a reckless way, giving a sort of grunt, which sometimes, for the life of me, I could not help accompanying with a groan that seemed to come from my very shoes. I had no fear of falling. In fact, I think I should have hailed it as a delightful change could we have rolled down a cliff and finished even life's journey with this one.

Lunch time found us in the midst of a pine forest, but such a sparsely grown one that the shade was a mockery. Heat, hunger, and those delightful insinuating little insects known as woodticks were not conducive to our happiness here, and more than glad were we when the arrival of our food bearer gave promise of an early change of scene.

We ate up everything we could, and then, with every nerve tingling with joy at the speedy home-coming, we mounted our faithful carriers for the last time.

Very soon after this we left the abominable but so-called wagon road, and took a short cut over the mountains. It would be but vain repetition to describe our "ups and downs" for the next few hours. The agony was just as exquisite, the scenery was just as grand and variable, but as far as I know it the English language contains no words of sufficient intensity to express more than I have already iterated and reiterated.

Presently a not far distant peak came in

sight, and as we clambered up higher we could see more and more of it until finally, on an elevated plateau at its base, there appeared a collection of houses. Across that intervening space I could gain no idea of what the village would be like, but I remember thinking that, with that glorious mountain to look at, I could never get homesick.

Here a rapidly approaching horseman came in view, who proved to be still another youth whom I had known in the States, and under this double escort I rode past a suburban mining camp, across the great *plaza* crowded with Sunday idlers, down another street, through a broad doorway into a paved courtyard, and found myself at last at home in *Yuscaran*.

Kind hands assisted me to dismount, and led me to the gallery-like corridor above, filled with friendly faces, and from there into a spacious parlor that seemed like a palace after my recent experiences.

In consideration of my fatigue I was almost immediately shown to my own

room, which I found luxuriously perfect
in all its appointments.

In the preceding six days I had learned
a good deal that was new, but it remained
for the revelation of this moment to teach
me what gratitude is. A wave of thank-
fulness came over me that sent me to my
knees, and ever since then I have been
content just to be glad I am alive.

Yes, my cousin, that mule was worse
than even you knew—infinitely worse than
a wheel, thanks to which I lost some twenty-
five pounds in six weeks, while in as many
days the mule reduced me to a mass of
lacerated skin, fractured bones, and mad-
dening flea-bites. Should you and my
gracious captain friend ever meet, may the
kindly Fates order my presence elsewhere !

But for the others I have no cheering
report of fulfilled predictions.

My complexion has been admired for its
fairness, a quality it still possesses—by
comparison ; I have searched long and
vainly among the surrounding inhabitants
for even one barbarian ; I have failed to

feel either sea-sickness or home-sickness; I have never been more perfectly healthy, and no dread fever seems to have selected me for a victim; I have found no snake coiled within my shoe of a morning, nor have I discovered one as an unwelcome bedfellow at night. Truth to tell, you are all wrong, but one, and now hear *me*.

Until railroads, flying machines, balloons, seven-league boots, magic wishing-rings, or some such means of transit are adopted in *Honduras*, I choose to stay here and grow up with the country, for *never*, while I have breath to object or heart to consider self, will I spend another six days "on the hurricane deck of a mule."

ALMIRA STILWELL COLE.